Also by elmo shade

Standing On One Leg: Poems of Love, Loss,
& the Spaces In-Between

Coffee Grinds: Mindful Poems & Stories
For the Less Than Perfect Soul

A Glorious Poetic Rage

the
dark side
of white bread

surviving our fathers

elmo shade

atmosphere press

Published by Atmosphere Press

Cover design by Ronaldo Alves

atmospherepress.com

For my mother
Lucy Doris Lafever
1927–1984

"He is like a stocking stuffed with things."

— The Father

Sharon Olds

Contents

Some Things in the Pocket of Someone I Loved

One of the first things I noticed
driving down my father's lengthy
front driveway, was him emerging
from an open garage door with
a bulging left shirt pocket,
a pocket protector toolbox stuffed
with pens, pencils, Kleenex, mini-
screwdrivers neatly tucked inside.
When I look beyond our years,
I see no apology for the messiness
left behind. Pencil lead in my
brother's back while playing guns
and knives, ink stains from leaky pens
on my arms shaped like 2-inch leather,
tissues my mother used to wipe tears
after his rage had ended, screwdrivers
the length of an index finger, each
with a thin tooth hooking them over
the top of his front pocket,
keeping them in their place,
keeping everything in its place.

The Childhood Years: 1952 - 1964

First Family Home
837 Alice Ave, Memphis, TN
1952

What Might Have Been

On a busy street corner,
a tall male figure sits
in an enclosed glass booth
and receives my vacation request:

How much are tickets?
When's the next performance?
Hello, did you hear me?

Looking back at four adults,
their fingers point at a ten-year-old.
A joke, some shaming humor
at my expense. Just a boy too
naive to notice the booth man was wax.

Just a boy too young to witness
his mother dying in smoker's lungs,
too dependent to run away from
the rage of a father, from a space
that rarely felt safe.

Just a boy trapped between uncomfortable laughter
and what might have been forgiveness.

Just a boy trapped   there still.

Not What You Wanted but What You Got

When   things get   quiet

      When   mothers try   to rescue   you

but can't   Shoved down   crawling out

      The smell of leather   the buckle   welts your skin

That's when   you wish   you had not been   born

        That's when   you wish   you had   a gun

Not   what you wanted   but what you   got

The Prodigal Son

Lucian Goodloe Weaver was my father's name. He grew up poor on a peach farm in Ripley, Tennessee, along with four brothers. His mother abandoned them when he was a young teen, and he became the adult for the first time. He had good looks and ripped arms. I'm not sure he ever experienced the playfulness of childhood.

His work ethic became evident on Saturday mornings when, after breakfast, all I desired as a kid was to watch cartoons on our black and white. He had other ideas. *Come on,* shouted as he walked out the back screen door, meant fetching things he needed when he needed them. He learned by doing, not by teaching. I never understood how someone could become so excited when it came time to changing the car oil and filter. He was always working.

I saw him cry only twice. The first after announcing at breakfast that I had quit my job, dropped out of my freshman year of college, and was leaving home the following morning with my best friend to travel West. When returning home after running out of money two months later, my mother burst into tears. My father was busy slamming doors. I wasn't the prodigal son his bible spoke of.

The last time was 10 years later. We were leaving the hospital together after my mother died. Standing in the parking lot, before walking to our separate vehicles, he broke down sobbing. It was in that moment I knew he had loved her. He softened somewhat after but being soft wasn't his persona. I don't think we ever understood each other.

elmo shade
October 2022

Grandfathers

His breath smelt awful of bourbon, his
clothes like chicory, like the stained
coffee mug on the dash of his 57 Ford
with a torn front vinyl seat.

I remember the ice cream he bought me,
a double scoop orange swirl and the hand-
rolled cigarette ash that dangled down
from his lower lip.

He would spit a chew when he thought
I wasn't looking. Even gasoline straight
from the can wasn't enough to clean earth
and nicotine from his nails.

My grandmother left him and her boys soon
after. I never saw him again. He died from
a broken liver and too much Jim Beam
but I didn't know who that was.

I dreamt of him long ago. He was tossing feed
to the chickens with one hand and pulling up
his beltless pants with the other. The ash looked
as though it had never left his lips.

And the other one? He died when my mother
was only 12 years old, before she inhaled
her first cigarette or had her first dance. Marshall
was his name and I don't say it enough.

House Arrest

Handcuffs are like quicksand, the harder
the struggle, the more trouble you're in.
He saved the famous ones used to snap
Machine Gun Kelly's wrists together in
the late 50s, and a lead-filled night stick,
lethal enough to kill a man with a single
slap to the head. He was working graveyard
shift so I waited before rummaging
through his top dresser drawer, forbidden
space for us kids. That night, I was the bad
guy, finding them without getting caught,
without suffering a single slap to the head.
Mother was half-asleep in the family room
watching a late show on the tele, sipping
bourbon & coke wrapped in a paper towel.
Tiptoeing into their bedroom, I slow opened
his drawer to see them, shining silver
with a keyhole on each cuff, hooked my right
index finger inside one and lifted them out.
My hands are kid-sized so slipping both
over my wrists was easy. I reached across
with opposite hands to tighten them snug
like he would with any bad guy. That's
when it hit me. The only key to unlock them
was fastened to his gun belt and off to work.
Mother must have heard me soaking up soap
to free myself. She struggled to hold back
her laughter. When my father arrived home
the next morning, he unlocked them without
speaking a word while I drifted back to sleep,
still in custody.

The Teenage Years: 1965 - 1971

Weaver Family 1937
(from left back row) Ward, Lorene, John Lewis
(from left front row) Lucian, Lemuel, Ray, Billy

This One Thing

i.

On weekends, my father and I would rise early,
sit silently at the kitchen table,
scars like grenade pins between our bodies.
It felt safe, if only for a moment. I love
the truth in this one thing—
the earth swallows up men and their anger.

ii.

He and I became the discarded ones, childhood
dreams disappearing in broken trust.
It is hard to believe when we were together,
our scars slowly softening, of a bond between us
severed so short.

iii.

Angels say fear is the cheapest room in the house.
Heroes die harder there.
They have no one left to save.
On weekends, I sit alone
at the kitchen table, remembering about his love—
or not.

Oscillation

He calls my name from the laundry room.
I rehearse my plea, "Just a little off the top, Pop".
The day before 5th grade pictures.
Sitting scared in his red Naugahyde chair.
My hair all grown out in mop-top fashion.
Over the ears completely covering my forehead.
Him looming behind me in a white V-neck.
Black-tooth comb in one hand.
A silver cutting blade in the other.
He runs the wet comb through my hair.
Combs it in the opposite direction.
The way He liked it, I guess.
The cut was slow. Like the turning of a fan.
Left side, now to right, then back again.
High and tight, worse than a combover.
I promised never to look this way again.
Gut sick. Puke rising in my throat.
I hated him. I hated what he had done.
I wake up from that at 5 a.m.
Scurry straight to the bathroom mirror.
Splash cold water on my face.
Stare at high and tight. Sixty years of age.
Maybe he was on to something.

You Could Have Stopped It, but You Didn't

Sending me off to school each morning with ashtray
kisses on my cheek.

You said you tried to quit but your early morning
coffee needed the company.

You could have stopped it, but you didn't.

The cigarette smoke in our kitchen was like heavy
fog hovering over Mount St Helens.

My school clothes reeked of exhales and your pink
lungs blackened with every inhale.

You could have stopped it, but you didn't.

Dying a young mother was no surprise. That lump
on your neck must have told you so.

Did the tobacco smoke blind you from seeing the raised
lumps on mine? Did you not hear the striking sounds?

You could have stopped it, but you didn't.

You died too soon. Fifty-six and cancer showed no
mercy. Did you remember me begging for some?

I felt like I was breathing on borrowed time.
You could have stopped loving me, but you didn't.

The Deer Hunter

The invitation was subtle. Lucian and two male
neighbors sitting out back drinking beers when
I heard my name called.

Our first night of deer hunting was about preparation.
Climbing into the deer stand, oiling and inspecting
shotguns and rifles, pitching tents, building a fire.

It was after dinner when I saw it —some type of horn
sitting on the picnic table not far from the smoke
of cigars and dirty jokes.

I walked over and noticed it had a mouthpiece facing
the same direction as the bell. A French horn, maybe.
It's a deer call. Only the deer can hear it.

Rising at 4 am to reach the deer stand before light.
It is cold and wet after a full night's rain. My wool
long underwear kept my small body warm.

We were in eye sight of the stand when I stepped in
it. A small ravine of rain water rising to my waist,
the sun rising, drying heat showing no mercy.

Try and remain still for hours sitting in a deer stand
with drying wet wool underwear. Misery of jock itch
kept the deer away and followed us back to camp.

When they weren't watching, I picked up the horn,
blew into the mouthpiece hard as my lungs allowed.
That's when white baby powder flew out over my face.

That was the last hunting trip I ever took with my father.
I thought once of taking my daughter. She might have
loved the hunt, but the laughter would have killed her.

The Adult Years: 1972 - 2011

The Brothers
(from left to right) Billy, Ray, Lemuel, Lucian, Ward

Father's Day, 1974

My grown male body lies
in fetal form. Sweat-soaked sheets.
Some stomach bug to blame.

I need my mother. No I need
her womb. To be back inside
without this pain.

This pain
walked to school with me.
Neck belt-buckled blistered.

Don't hurt him, she screamed.
Hurts me more than it hurts you.
That's what he always said.

Claw through carpet to call her,
beg her to bring the bottled brew,
medicine to help me sleep.

I awaken late afternoon lying
on the kitchen floor, a pillow under
my head.

See him seated beside me,
where he had been all day, holding
my medicine and a spoon.

I Would Run Everybody Out

Sometimes I imagine a Coffee House where the Baristas and Grinders were old friends or family and everyone who entered to sip were old friends, as well. What a treat it would be if my mother was preparing a triple cortado and my grandfather serving it on a vintage platter.

I would buy a round for Gail and Beth and Karen and Frank and all the others that I had hurt, disappointed, judged or abandoned as a younger man and I would have Billy and Jennifer and Denice split the bill to pay for being part of the Hurting Team with me.

I would invite all my former in-laws to pull up a chair and send sign language of forgiveness under the table since none of us were willing to forgive when older tables tumbled over sideways from death and divorce.

I would move my grandsons' chairs next to me, one on the left and one on the right, and tell them how fortunate they are to have a family's love, courage, and commitment to raise them to be respectful of others.

And I would ask Lucian to sweep and mop the floor, clean up any remaining trash I have been carrying for too long. Then I would run everybody out, lock the doors, sit down with him, and have the conversation we never had.

The Box

They said I could have them, boxed
glass containers stored in the attic
after our mother died. My stepmom
walked with me up the wooden staircase
leaving Lucian comfortably below
lounging in his living room recliner.

I pull down on the light cord and see
a metal bed frame, old family portraits,
bicycle training wheels, scattered cardboard
on plywood sheets. *There they are,* she said
pointing to a box near an old set of Samsonite.

I step over a worn travel bag, plant my left
foot on an attic rafter, then reach down
to retrieve the box. My right foot misses
the rafter then plunges completely through
the sheet rock into the living room.

I see an image of my father's head below.
Insulation particles float down like pink
snowflakes covering his thin, gray hair.

Careful to rise, I retrieve the box, slow walk
down the staircase like a ten-year-old caught
rummaging through his dresser drawer.

Gently dusting insulation from his shoulders
and before *I'm sorry* could leave my lips, he offers
four words I never expected to hear—

Are you alright, son?

The Hospice Years: 2012 - 2014

Lucian 1937

Unbuckled No Longer

His breath sour
like curdled milk
spilled over my face.
His eyes closed, skin
ashen like smoke,
leukemia lingers in a
bloated body. Hospice
says, *Time is short.*

I reach under arms,
once muscular and
massive, now fragile
like our faces close
enough to kiss, the stench
of stomach acid rises in my throat.

His body a heavy lift up
and out of the recliner
into a cold, metal bed as
a sudden muffled moan
manifests into memory
of a boy's welted neck.

As I release him down
into sleep, not to disturb
his dream, he cries for
a younger son. His belt
no longer unbuckled.

No Refund

I had paid a week's wages to attend a silent retreat located
in the northern hills of California. It was my respite from
the busyness of my mind. Seven silent days without phones or screens.

The leukemia chemo had stopped working. Doctors told us so.
His clock had begun ticking like the World War II bomb
he helped defuse. But with bags packed and boarding pass
pre-printed, I was ready to depart.

That's when I received the call saying he will likely slip
into "the death coma" within 48 hours. I sat my phone
down and took a long breath, noticing the irony in all of this,
i.e. walking a labyrinth or watching his chest rise and fall.

When my wife and I arrived back home, he was sitting up
in his electric recliner, feet protruding out from the end
of a Winnie the Pooh blanket. Hospice said to gift him
goodbyes before morphine rendered him unconscious.

One by one, family gathered around him. First the grandkids,
then the adults. I took a photo of my wife seated next to him,
unaware that she would be dead from cancer in 18 months.

The following morning, I received a message that my request
for a retreat refund had been denied, like the morphine he refused
to swallow just hours before. Walking to his bed, his mouth agape,
I felt no pulse. He was gone. I sensed he knew I was not.

The Letter

Dear Lucian:

This is only the second letter I have ever written to you. The first was over 30 years ago. My therapist thought it would bring me some peace from childhood pain. Her assignment was simple: write a letter addressed to you, present day, and pour out whatever my heart needed to pour out. She wasn't specific, which I appreciated. I remember writing how confused I was, as a child, to understand why you were so angry, why you spewed so much rage when I only wanted to be loved and accepted.

I watched as you opened the letter, tearing the envelope unevenly at one end, and for the next few frozen moments, waited for your response. When there was none, I asked, *Do you have anything to say?* You dropped the single sheet of paper onto the breakfast table and without hesitation, said, *Boy, you have always been too sensitive.*

That was not the response I was expecting, but it was the response I got. And that was it. We never spoke about the letter again or what it might have meant to you. It was as though the moment never happened. That defined how most of the difficult conversations in our household were handled. If you don't talk about it, it never happened.

But you were right. I was sensitive. I was never the man you wanted me to be, e.g. manly, macho, gruff, dirt under my fingernails from changing car oil or installing new brake pads. I never liked skinning a squirrel you had killed while hunting or sitting in a deer stand freezing my ass off. I really wanted to watch mother scramble an egg or learn how to make her signature potato salad.

There were good moments. The fly baseballs you hit behind our house with one arm while catching the ball with the other, our camping trips in the Ozarks, the down payment on my first new car (even though you somehow convinced me not to order a radio or air conditioner), the buzz saw that I never used, the rescue from my night in hell, and the early morning sausage and biscuits wrapped in a paper towel, warmed in the microwave, always to go.

When I finally left Memphis in middle age, you visited once in 15 years. I was only 3 hours away. After your passing, my stepmom said you did not feel welcome. Maybe it was the phone calls I never answered or my short visits home before I had to leave. The truth is you were always welcome. If regret is wishing you could have a better past, I have only two. That I had encouraged you more often to come. That I had sat down to eat my sausage and biscuit.

With love,

elmo

The Afterlife: 2015 - 2022

Memphis Police Department 1949

When a Hurricane Released the Caged Roosters of Kauai

He comes into the world
strikingly colorful,
swaggers with a twist,
tells me how he survived,
how the storm emptied the cages,
scattered his feathers and fowl
over the island. It is 3 a.m.
He refuses to sleep like my
restless legs begging to
follow him, free of pain,
free of captivity, of not knowing
when the hatchet will fall,
spill his blood red like his wattle,
like welts on the skin of something
so innocent.

instructions from his thanksgiving recipe

clouds gather over wet sand
mist blows in from ocean waves
thaw turkey trim fat from rear and wash
gulls walk briskly until the labradors
chase them down the shoreline
forcing each to take flight
cold rain blows into my face
I cannot see what is real what is true
place in oval pan 12x17x4 inches deep
wind chaps my neck my naked hands
numbs them from not knowing why
this moment seems surreal I exhale
invite blindness to return with the tide
yellow stained paper instructions written
in my father's hand *rub lots of salt to*
taste the seasoning of times past I inhale
ocean air waves crash closer to the shore
gulls disappear like loved ones carried away
spread all over turkey real good
I sink my knees into sand giving thanks

Rapid Eye Movement

In my adult dreams, I'm never able to escape —es

I am the opposite of all packed and nowhere to go.
Skin-knuckled panicked.
I don't recognize this terrain at all. It is foreign to me.
Campsites, strewn supplies, humans without faces.
Try and fit a chest of drawers into the back of a VW
or climb up the side of a pirate ship on a roped fishnet.
Boarding time is less than one-hour and I've packed nothing.
Am I driving or flying?
The high school reunion crowd next to my campsite is dressed to the
    nines.
Why didn't I get the memo?
All the men have white mustaches or beards.
All the women have short hair and round faces.
They look safe but have trouble remembering what day it is.
If I don't wake up before they leave, I'll never make the flight

home

    why would I want to go back?

I am all packed with anywhere to go. I need to run away.
Get out of here.
But the plane is boarding.
Why is he always so angry with me? I'm just a boy who loves his mother
Just a boy too late to wander off of the reservation.
The escarpment too high for a first-born.
I suddenly remember I don't have to report for roll call at the South
    Precinct.
That's why I was camping far away from

him

    rescuing me was an act of love.

Lost in the Smokey Mountains of Tennessee while gathering firewood.
Just a boy and his little brother.
I hear Lucian's whistle, the one that always meant *get your ass home now.*
Follow the whistle, not the woods.
I can make the flight before the gate closes.

Need to hurry now.
I'm always running off and leaving more than I ever catch up to.
I want to go back to the campground.
Not the one with the whistle.
I can't leave until I find my wallet. There's no app for that on my iPhone.
I'm f'd.

The Dark Side of White Bread

He passed quietly, surrounded
by family, wearing his white
V-neck tee, feet covered in
pink hospice socks. I could
have asked for them or maybe
a collared shirt, a bolo tie,
a cap, something carrying
his scent. But I did not. His
death was expected. Leukemia
gave him less than 3 years. He
robbed it of every month. I did
not see him take his final breath
like I did with my wife, Tracy.
Nor did I lay my head down on
his chest when it failed to rise.
Just hours before, I was on duty
throughout the night, sitting with
him, holding a morphine spoon.
An unexpected role reversal from
forty years ago in my kitchen, him
holding a spoon for me. How can
love be so different for the two
of them —a wife, a father? How tears
for one can be tears without for another.
He loved me the only way he knew —
to have a good laugh, to make turkey
and mayo sandwiches on white bread,
to pick up the tab.

Acknowledgements

Maybe We Could Run Everybody Out; *Coffee Grinds: Mindful Poems & Stories for the Less Than Perfect Soul*; Amazon Books; 2019 (Revised)

Some Things in The Pocket of Someone I Loved; *Coffee Grinds: Mindfulness Poems & Stories for the Less Than Perfect Soul*; Amazon Books; 2019; (Revised)

Not What You Wanted but What You Got; *A Glorious Poetic Rage*; Atmosphere Press; 2021

Author/poet credits

What Might Have Been; *the dark side of white bread: surviving our fathers*; Atmosphere Press; 2023; R. Bragg, —*All Over But The Shoutin'*; Vintage Books; 1997

This One Thing; *the dark side of white bread: surviving our fathers;* Atmosphere Press; 2023; R. Hayden, —*Those Winter Sundays;* Yehuda Amichai, —*In the Middle of This Century*

Special thanks

To Ana Michalowsky, my poetry coach & mentor, whose guidance and editing expertise throughout the entire manuscript was invaluable.

To my friend and cigar aficionado, Pat Currin, for his poetry collection title suggestion, *The Dark Side of White Bread.*

To Claudia Savage, Jim Bellar, & Armin Tolentino, fellow poets & authors, who invested their valuable time providing back cover reviews and suggested edits for this chapbook.

About Atmosphere Press

Atmosphere Press is an independent, full-service publisher for excellent books in all genres and for all audiences. Learn more about what we do at atmospherepress.com.

We encourage you to check out some of Atmosphere's latest releases, which are available at Amazon.com and via order from your local bookstore:

Melody in Exile, by S.T. Grant

Covenant, by Kate Carter

Near Scattered Praise Lies Our Substantial Endeavor, by Ron Penoyer

Weightless, Woven Words, by Umar Siddiqui

Journeying: Flying, Family, Foraging, by Nicholas Ranson

Lexicon of the Body, by DM Wallace

Controlling Chaos, by Michael Estabrook

Almost a Memoir, by M.C. Rydel

Throwing the Bones, by Caitlin Jackson

Like Fire and Ice, by Eli

Sway, by Tricia Johnson

A Patient Hunger, by Skip Renker

Lies of an Indispensable Nation: Poems About the American Invasions of Iraq and Afghanistan, by Lilvia Soto

The Carcass Undressed, by Linda Eguiliz

Poems That Wrote Me, by Karissa Whitson

Gnostic Triptych, by Elder Gideon

For the Moment, by Charnjit Gill

Battle Cry, by Jennifer Sara Widelitz

I woke up to words today, by Daniella Deutsch

Never Enough, by William Guest

Second Adolescence, by Joe Rolnicki

About the Author

elmo shade is an accredited Certified Mindfulness Teacher-Professional (CMT-P) through the International Mindfulness Teachers Association (IMTA). He is an author of three additional poetry collections: *Standing On One Leg: Poems of Love, Loss, & the Spaces In-Between* (2017), *Coffee Grinds – Mindful Poems and Stories for the Less Than Perfect Soul* (2019), and *A Glorious Poetic Rage* (2021). He lives and writes in the Pacific Northwest and is an unabashed fan of Double IPAs, Opus-X Cigars, & RUSH.

Lightning Source UK Ltd.
Milton Keynes UK
UKHW010634160123
415428UK00005B/261

9 781639 887200